Lerner SPORTS

SPORTS VIPs

MEET KEVIN DURANT

JOE LEVIT

Lerner Publications ◆ Minneapolis

Lerner Publications Company
An imprint of Lerner Publishing Group, Inc.
241 First Avenue North
Minneapolis, MN 55401 USA

For reading levels and more information, look up this title at www.lernerbooks.com.

Main body text set in Aptifer Slab LT Pro. Typeface provided by Linotype AG.

Editor: Brianna Kaiser **Designer:** Kimberly Morales
Lerner team: Sue Marquis

Library of Congress Cataloging-in-Publication Data

Names: Levit, Joseph author.
Title: Meet Kevin Durant / Joe Levit.
Description: Minneapolis, MN : Lerner Publications Company, [2023] | Series: Sports VIPs | Includes bibliographical references and index. | Audience: Ages 7–11 | Audience: Grades 4–6 | Summary: "Basketball forward Kevin Durant has twice won the NBA Finals with the Golden State Warriors. Sports fans will thrill in learning about the MVP's greatest moments both on and off the court"— Provided by publisher.
Identifiers: LCCN 2021043615 (print) | LCCN 2021043616 (ebook) | ISBN 9781728458137 (library binding) | ISBN 9781728463322 (paperback) | ISBN 9781728462301 (ebook)
Subjects: LCSH: Durant, Kevin, 1988—Juvenile literature. | Basketball players—United States—Biography—Juvenile literature.
Classification: LCC GV884.D868 L48 2023 (print) | LCC GV884.D868 (ebook) | DDC 796.323092 [B]—dc23

LC record available at https://lccn.loc.gov/2021043615
LC ebook record available at https://lccn.loc.gov/2021043616

Manufactured in the United States of America
1-50843-50180-1/28/2022

TABLE OF CONTENTS

CRUSHING THE CAVALIERS

In 2017, the Golden State Warriors faced the Cleveland Cavaliers in the National Basketball Association (NBA) Finals for the third year in a row. The Warriors beat the Cavs in the 2015 Finals 4–2. The next year, the Warriors had the best regular-season record in NBA history.

Then they had a 3–1 lead in the Finals. But LeBron James and the Cavs came roaring back to take the next three games. In 2016–2017, all-star forward Kevin Durant joined the Warriors. Adding Durant to the team made all the difference in the Finals.

FAST FACTS

DATE OF BIRTH: September 29, 1988
POSITION: small forward
LEAGUE: NBA

PROFESSIONAL HIGHLIGHTS: won gold medals in basketball at the 2012, 2016, and 2020 Olympic Games; is an 11-time NBA All-Star; won two NBA championships

PERSONAL HIGHLIGHTS: was Most Valuable Player (MVP) of the 2006 McDonald's All-American Game; was Naismith College Player of the Year in 2007; became part owner of a major-league soccer team

Kevin Durant takes a shot for the Warriors during Game 3 of the 2017 NBA Finals.

In Game 1, Durant racked up 38 points, eight rebounds, and eight assists. In Game 4, he scored 31 points. He sealed the Warriors' victory by sinking a three-point shot with 45 seconds left in the game. And in Game 5, he helped close the Finals 4–1 with 39 points, seven rebounds, and five assists.

It was Durant's first NBA Finals win. And the awards didn't stop there. He was also named Finals MVP.

Durant holds up his MVP trophy during a victory parade for the Warriors in June 2017.

CHAPTER 1

A STAR FROM THE START

Kevin Durant was born on September 29, 1988. He lived near Washington, DC, with his mother, Wanda Durant, and his grandmother Barbara Davis. He has three siblings: Tony, Rayvonne, and Brianna.

Kevin's father, Wayne Pratt, left the family when Kevin was very young. Durant admired his mother for her support while he was growing up. "You made us believe," he later said. "You sacrificed for us. You the real MVP." Kevin later reconnected with his dad when he was a teenager. They traveled to basketball tournaments together.

Durant and his mom, Wanda Durant (*left*), in 2011

Kevin played high school basketball for three different teams. Before his senior year at Montrose Christian School, he was already 6 feet 7 (2 m). At the end of the season, he was named the *Washington Post* All-Met Boys' Basketball Player of the Year. He was also named the MVP of the 2006 McDonald's All-American Game. Many considered him the second-best high school player of 2006.

SUPER SPORTS SCOOP

Kevin was fascinated with weather as a kid. His childhood interest later inspired him to name his shoes the Nike KD 4 Weatherman. The shoes even had a matching shirt. "I always wanted to be a weatherman growing up," Durant said when the sneakers came out in 2011.

In March 2006, Kevin (*right*) plays in the McDonald's All-American Game.

After high school, Durant went to the University of Texas. He played for the Longhorns in the 2006–2007 season. He led the team to a fourth seed in the East Regional conference of the 2007 National Collegiate Athletic Association (NCAA) tournament. The Longhorns lost in the second round. But Durant scored 30 points and made nine rebounds in that game.

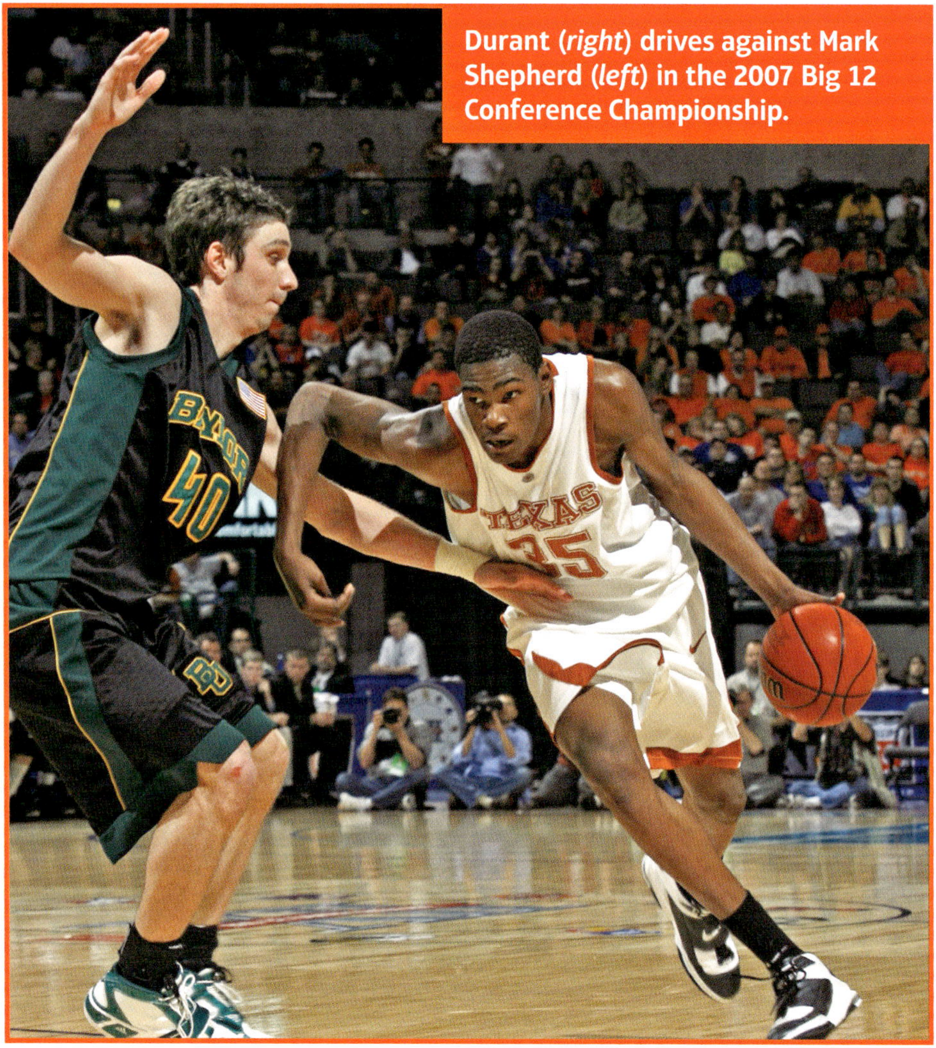

Durant (*right*) drives against Mark Shepherd (*left*) in the 2007 Big 12 Conference Championship.

That year, he became the first freshman to win the Naismith College Player of the Year award. This award is given to the top male and female NCAA basketball player each year. After only one year in college, Durant was ready for the NBA.

CHAPTER 2

BRINGING THE THUNDER

The Seattle SuperSonics couldn't wait to add Durant to their team. They selected him second overall in the 2007 NBA draft. Durant proved they made the right choice. He averaged 20 points per game in his first season as a pro. At the time, only two other teenagers had matched that feat—Carmelo Anthony and LeBron James. Durant easily took home the NBA Rookie of the Year award.

Before Durant's second season, the team moved. Durant then starred for the Oklahoma City Thunder. In the 2009–2010 season, he was selected to his first All-Star Game and averaged 30.1 points per game. At 21, that made him the youngest scoring champion ever. The Thunder made the playoffs but lost to the Los Angeles Lakers in the first round in six games.

Durant dunks in a game in 2009.

Durant signed a five-year, $86 million contract extension before the 2010–2011 season. He again led the NBA in scoring, this time with 27.7 points per game. But the Thunder lost to the Dallas Mavericks in the Western Conference Finals. The Mavericks went on to win the championship. A year later, Durant was the scoring champion again. He led the Thunder all the way to the Finals. There, they lost to the Miami Heat 4–1.

Durant drives toward the basket for the Thunder during the NBA Playoffs in 2010.

That summer, Durant played for Team USA at the Olympic Games in London, England. They had an 8–0 record to win the gold medal. Durant had the highest scoring average on the team with 19.5 points per game.

In 2012–2013, the Thunder had a 60–22 regular-season record. They were the top-ranked team in the Western Conference. But the team struggled in the playoffs. They lost in the semifinals to the Memphis Grizzlies 4–1.

SUPER SPORTS SCOOP

In May 2013, a powerful tornado went through Moore, Oklahoma. The tornado harmed many homes, buildings, and people. Durant joined the relief effort. He donated $1 million to help the community.

Durant (*center*) and Russell Westbrook (*right*) celebrate Team USA beating Spain to win the gold medal at the 2012 Olympic Games.

The next season, Durant passed NBA star Michael Jordan to set a new record for games in a row with at least 25 points (41). But the Thunder exited the Western Conference Finals after losing to the San Antonio Spurs 4–2. The Thunder failed to make the playoffs the next year because Durant was injured for much of the season.

Exercising helps Durant stay in shape and excel on the court each season. He does leg exercises such as lunges and squats to keep his legs strong. Sometimes he works out with medicine balls. These are weighted balls used to build strength. Durant makes sure to eat healthful foods.

Stretching before games and practices helps Durant keep his muscles healthy and avoid injury.

Durant works on his shooting during practices.

Durant has deals with companies such as Nike and Gatorade. He even appeared in a series of Foot Locker commercials. In one commercial, people are trying to find a man who made dangerous dunks. But nobody suspected Durant since he was the nicest guy in the NBA.

CHAPTER 3

JOINING A CHAMPION

In 2015–2016, the Thunder made it back to the Western Conference Finals. By Game 5, the Thunder was up 3–1. But the Golden State Warriors rallied. They had three straight wins and advanced to the NBA Finals.

Durant was eager to get back to the Finals. He still wanted an NBA championship. But Durant and the Thunder couldn't beat the Warriors. So in the 2016 off-season, he signed a contract to join the Warriors. Many fans and basketball experts felt he took the easy way out by joining the Warriors instead of beating them. "He chose to go against Andre Iguodala and Draymond Green, two elite defenders, in practices rather than in Western Conference finals games," *Sports Illustrated* writer Ben Golliver said.

On May 18, 2016, Durant (*center*) helped the Thunder beat the Warriors 118–91 in Game 2 of the Western Conference Finals.

SUPER SPORTS SCOOP

Durant helped Team USA win the gold medal in men's basketball at the 2016 Olympics in Rio de Janeiro, Brazil. Durant was the team's high scorer again. He averaged 19.4 points per game.

But Durant knew joining the Warriors was the right decision. "It really pains me to know that I will disappoint so many people with this choice, but I believe I am doing what I feel is the right thing at this point in my life and my playing career," Durant said.

In the 2017 playoffs, Durant helped the Warriors to a record 12–0 start in the playoffs. He averaged 35.2 points per game in the Finals, helping the Warriors win the championship.

The following year, he came up big in Game 7 of the Western Conference Finals. His 34 points against the Houston Rockets sent the Warriors to the NBA Finals again. There, they met the Cleveland Cavaliers for the fourth straight season. The Warriors swept the Cavaliers 4–0. Durant won Finals MVP for the second year in a row.

Durant drives to the basket during Game 7 of the 2017 Western Conference Finals.

CHAPTER 4

NEXT MOVES

In 2018–2019, Durant scored career playoff highs of 45 and 50 points in games against the Los Angeles Clippers. During Game 5 of the NBA semifinals, he strained his right calf. He missed the rest of the Western Conference playoffs, but the Warriors made it to the NBA Finals

Durant returned for Game 5 of the Finals. He soon tore his right Achilles tendon. This tendon is a tissue that connects the calf muscles to the bones of the heel. His season was over. Without him, the Warriors lost 4–2 to the Toronto Raptors. Durant was traded to the Brooklyn Nets after the season. He missed the entire 2019–2020 season to focus on healing his injury.

Durant plays for the Brooklyn Nets in 2021.

SUPER SPORTS SCOOP

Basketball is not the only pro sport that Durant is involved with. In 2020, he became a part owner of the Philadelphia Union. It's a major-league soccer team.

In 2020–2021, Durant teamed up with Kyrie Irving and James Harden in Brooklyn. They earned the second seed in the East. In the conference semifinals, they met the third seed Milwaukee Bucks.

In Game 5, Durant had 49 points, 17 rebounds, and 10 assists in a comeback win. "This is a signature performance for Kevin and it was beautiful to watch," said Brooklyn coach Steve Nash. In Game 7, Durant poured in 48 more points. But the Bucks won the game, series, and eventually the NBA title.

The spread of COVID-19 caused the 2020 Tokyo Olympics to be played in 2021. Durant helped Team USA to another gold medal. Durant is a basketball superstar. Fans look forward to seeing what he will do next.

Devin Booker (*left*) and Durant (*right*) wear their gold medals during a ceremony at the Tokyo Olympics.

KEVIN DURANT CAREER STATS

GAMES PLAYED:

904

POINTS PER GAME:

27.1

REBOUNDS PER GAME:

7.1

ASSISTS PER GAME:

4.2

BLOCKS PER GAME:

1.1

STEALS PER GAME:

1.1

GLOSSARY

assist: a pass that leads directly to a score

conference: a group of teams in the NBA

draft: when teams take turns choosing new players

playoffs: where NBA teams compete with one another for the chance to win a title

rebound: grabbing and controlling a basketball after a missed shot

seed: a team's ranking in a tournament

semifinals: a round of a tournament before the finals

tournament: a series of contests played for a championship

SOURCE NOTES

9 Agustin Mojica, "Kevin Durant Reconnected with His Father after Being Abandoned by Him," Sportscasting, July 21, 2020, https://www.sportscasting.com/kevin-durant-reconnected-with-his-father-after-being-abandoned-by-him/.

10 Jason Samenow, "Nike Weatherman Shoes by Kevin Durant: A Hot, Electrifying Forecast for Your Feet," *Washington Post*, December 9, 2011, https://www.washingtonpost.com/blogs/capital-weather-gang/post/nike-weatherman-shoes-by-kevin-durant-a-hot-electrifying-forecast-for-your-feet/2011/12/08/gIQA3qRUiO_blog.html.

21 Ben Golliver, "Golden Decision: Kevin Durant Shakes Up the NBA with Move to the Warriors," *Sports Illustrated*, July 4, 2016, https://www.si.com/nba/2016/07/04/kevin-durant-warriors-free-agency-stephen-curry-russell-westbrook.

22 Kevin Durant, "My Next Chapter," Players' Tribune, July 4, 2016, https://www.theplayerstribune.com/articles/kevin-durant-nba-free-agency-announcement.

26 Chris Milholen and Matthew Brooks, "Kevin Durant Puts on Historic Performance to Lead Nets Past Bucks in Game 5, 114–108," SB Nation, June 16, 2021, https://www.netsdaily.com/2021/6/16/22535877/kevin-durant-puts-on-historic-performance-to-lead-nets-past-bucks-in-game-5-114-108.

LEARN MORE

Basketball—*Sports Illustrated Kids*
https://www.sikids.com/basketball

Brooklyn Nets Official Site
https://www.nba.com/nets/

Kevin Durant—Britannica Kids
https://kids.britannica.com/students/article/Kevin-Durant/629892

Levit, Joe. *Basketball's G.O.A.T.: Michael Jordan, LeBron James, and More.* Minneapolis: Lerner Publications, 2020.

Monson, James. *Behind the Scenes Basketball*. Minneapolis: Lerner Publications, 2020.

Wetzel, Dan. *Kevin Durant*. New York: Henry Holt, 2020.

INDEX

PHOTO ACKNOWLEDGMENTS

Image credits: AP Photo/Eric Gay, p. 4; Ronald Martinez/Getty Images, p. 6; Michael Macor/The San Francisco Chronicle/Getty Images, p. 7; Jim Redman/WireImage/Getty Images, p. 8; AP Photo/Sue Ogrocki, p. 9; AP Photo/Denis Poroy, p. 11; Larry Smith/Icon SMI/Icon Sport Media/Getty Images, p. 12; AP Photo/Kevin P. Casey, p. 13; Albert Pena/Icon SMI/Corbis/Icon Sportswire/Getty Images, p. 14; Dilip Vishwanat/Getty Images, p. 15; Christian Petersen/Getty Images, p. 17; Ron Elkman/Sports Imagery/Getty Images, p. 18; Ethan Miller/Getty Images, p. 19; AP Photo/Eric Gay, p. 20; AP Photo/Marcio Jose Sanchez, p. 21; AP Photo/David Phillip, p. 23; AP Photo//Ben Margot, p. 24; Will Newton /Getty Images, p. 25; AP Photo/Charlie Neibergall, p. 27.

Cover image: AP Photo/Matt Slocum.